# Grasslands

## By Duncan Scheff

**Steadwell Books**

Raintree Steck-Vaughn Publishers

A Harcourt Company

Austin · New York
www.steck-vaughn.com

Published by Raintree Steck-Vaughn Publishers,
an imprint of Steck-Vaughn Company.

**Library of Congress Cataloging-in-Publication Data**
Cataloging-in-Publication data is available upon request.
ISBN 0-7398-3562-9

10 9 8 7 6 5 4 3 2 W 04 03 02 01

**Produced by Compass Books**

**Photo Acknowledgments**
Corbis, cover
Digital Stock Photos/title page, 5, 13, 19, 20, 23, 26
Photo Network, 8
Visuals Unlimited, 14, 17; Pat Armstrong, 11; Edward Hodgson, 24, 28

**Content Consultants**
Susan L. Woodward
Professor of Geography
Radford University
Radford, Virginia

Maria Kent Rowell
Science Consultant
Sebastopol, California

David Larwa
National Science Education Consultant
Educational Training Services
Brighton, Michigan

# CONTENTS

Zebras have adapted to live in the grasslands of Africa.

# THE GRASSLANDS BIOME

Some scientists study parts of Earth called biomes. Biomes are large regions, or areas, that have communities of plants and animals. A community is a group of plants and animals that live in the same place. Grasslands are a biome.

Each biome has a different **climate**. Climate is the usual weather in a place. Climate includes wind speeds, amount of rainfall, and temperature. Temperature measures how hot or cold a place is.

Different biomes have different kinds of soils. Many kinds of plants grow in biomes with rich soil. Fewer plants grow in biomes with dry, poor, or wind-blown soil.

Plants and animals are **adapted** to their biomes. To be adapted means that a living thing has features that help it fit where it lives.

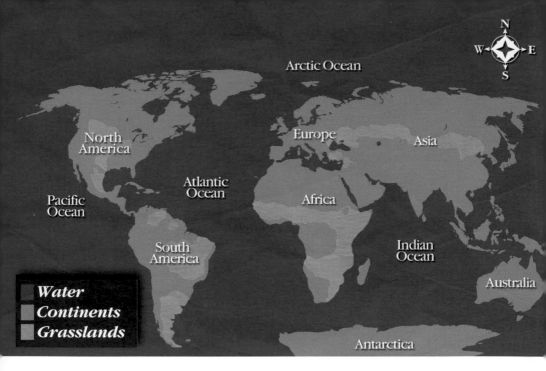

Arctic Ocean

North
America

Europe

Asia

Atlantic
Ocean

Pacific
Ocean

Africa

South
America

Indian
Ocean

Australia

Antarctica

■ Water
■ Continents
■ Grasslands

## Grasslands

Grasslands are mainly grassy plains. A plain is a wide, flat area with few or no trees. Grasses and small shrubs are the main plants that grow on grasslands.

Many grasslands have fairly dry climates with strong winds. The wind blows the grasses and makes them move. The movement looks like waves. That is why some people call grasslands "seas of grass."

Grasslands cover around 30% of Earth's land. Every continent except Antarctica has grasslands.

A continent is one of the seven large bodies of land on Earth.

Grasslands form in certain latitude bands. A latitude band is an area of land a certain distance from the **equator**. The equator is an imaginary line that divides Earth into a northern and a southern half.

There are two kinds of grasslands. Each kind of grassland has a different climate. Tropical grasslands form in a tropical latitude band near the equator. Tropical grasslands are hot all year with a dry season and a rainy season. Temperate grasslands form in latitude bands above and below the tropical latitude. These grasslands are warm in summer and cold in winter. In temperate grasslands, it rains or snows throughout the year.

Grasslands have different names in different parts of the world. Prairies are grasslands found in North America. South America's grasslands are called savannas and pampas. Africa's grasslands are also called savannas. Europe and Asia have grasslands called steppes. Savannas are tropical. Prairies, pampas, and steppes are temperate.

This grassland has a few small hills and mainly short grasses.

# About Grasslands

Grasslands are mostly flat with some low hills. They often form in dry places in the middle of continents. Grasslands are often located between mountains and deserts.

Grasslands may form on one side of a mountain. Mountains receive much more rain than the places around them. Storms usually travel from west to east over mountains. Air cools as it travels up a mountain. The cool air forms rainclouds. The rain falls on the mountain. The air becomes much drier by the time it passes over the mountain. This makes places to the east of mountains very dry and windy. Many trees do not grow well in a dry climate. But grasses and small plants can grow well there.

# Fire

Fire is important to the growth of grasslands. Fire warms the top layer of the soil. It burns old, dead plants so new plants can grow. By burning plants, nutrients are added to the soil. A nutrient is something that helps living things grow. Plants need nutrients from soil to grow.

Fire also helps keep trees from growing on grasslands. Fire burns down huge areas of plants, including any tall trees. Grasses are not killed. After a fire, grasses begin to grow again. But trees take a long time to grow. Fire usually burns the grassland again before trees can grow tall.

# Soil

The best soil on temperate grasslands is called black earth. Black earth is light soil with large air spaces. It can hold a lot of water. Black earth is rich in **humus**. Humus is made mainly of rotting plants and some animal remains. Humus is rich in nutrients. Plants grow easily in black earth. Nutrients stay near the surface where plants' roots can get them.

**Lightning is the most common cause of grassland fires.**

Brown prairie soil covers grasslands that receive less rain. The soil has less humus than black earth. But plants still grow well.

Red earth is sandy, dusty soil. This brown-red soil covers tropical grasslands. The warm climate makes plants rot very quickly so they do not add much humus to the soil. Plants do not grow as well in red earth as they do in other soils.

# Climate

All grasslands are semiarid. Semiarid means that the climate is dry, but not as dry as deserts. Grasslands receive 10 to 50 inches (25 to 127 cm) of rain each year. The amount of rainfall determines what kind of grassland it will be.

Tropical grasslands are the wettest kind of grassland. They have a winter dry season and a summer rainy season. Little rain falls during the winter. But tropical grasslands may receive 20 to 50 inches (51 to 127 cm) of rain during summer.

Tropical grasslands have warm temperatures throughout the year. The average summer temperature is about 80° Fahrenheit (27° C). The average winter temperature is about 65° Fahrenheit (18° C).

Temperate grasslands receive less rain than tropical grasslands. About 10 to 30 inches (25 to 76 cm) of rain or snow fall there each year. Most of this falls during spring and early summer. Temperate climates sometimes have **droughts**. A drought is a long time without rain or snow.

Temperate grasslands have a cold season and a hot season. Summer temperatures can climb to

**Tornadoes most often strike grasslands in the Great Plains area of North America.**

more than 100° Fahrenheit (38° C). Temperatures often fall below −10° Fahrenheit (-23° C) in winter.

Strong storms can strike grasslands. During droughts, strong winds form dust storms that blow dust around. Tornadoes also sweep across the plains. A tornado's spinning winds blow at speeds of more than 300 miles (483 km) an hour.

These plants are sedges. They usually grow near water.

# GRASSLAND PLANTS

Grasses are the most common grassland plants. The tallest grasses grow in tropical grasslands where it is wetter. Temperate grasslands usually have much shorter grasses. It is drier there.

Sedges are plants that look much like grasses. But sedges need more water than grasses. They often grow in damp places along the edges of ponds or streams.

Forbs are small plants with wide leaves and bright flowers. They do not have woody stems like trees and shrubs. Sunflowers, mints, and goldenrod are common forbs in temperate grasslands. Forbs can live up to 50 years.

# How Plants Survive

Plants that live in grasslands have adapted to the grassland climate. They are able to live through dry times and grow back after fires.

Grassland plants have adapted to live with little water. Some plants store water in their stems. Other plants, such as forbs, have very deep roots. The roots may grow 20 feet (6 m) down into the soil. The different grasses and plants send their roots down to different layers of soil to find water. This way, all the different kinds of plants can find water.

Grassland plants are able to live through common fires. Grasses are well suited to grow back after fires. Up to 75% of a grass plant lives underground. The top of the plant burns in the fire. But the roots are safe underground. So, the top of the plant can quickly grow back after fire.

Some plants lie dormant for part of the year. Dormant means alive, but not growing. Special underground plant parts rest during the long, dry season. They start growing again during the short, wet season.

**More than 300 kinds of plants grow on grasslands.**

Lions are predators. Predators catch and eat other animals. Lions hunt many different kinds of prey. Prey are animals eaten by other animals.

# GRASSLAND ANIMALS

Many large herbivores live on grasslands. A herbivore is an animal that eats only plants. Many herbivores, such as deer and rabbits, are grazers. Grazers eat grasses and other plants. Buffalo, elephants, horses, kangaroos, and antelope are grazers.

Carnivores also live on grasslands. These animals hunt and eat other animals. Snakes, owls, and hawks are carnivores. Lions and tigers eat herbivores, such as zebras and antelope.

Reptiles also live on grasslands. These are cold-blooded animals. The blood in cold-blooded animals warms or cools to about the same temperature as the air or water around them. Grassland reptiles include snakes and lizards.

**These spotted hyenas are scavengers. They eat dead animals that they did not kill.**

## How Animals Survive

Grassland animals must be able to live through dry times. Many animals migrate. Migrate means to move from place to place. They leave to find food and water during the dry season. They return during the rainy season when food and water are easy to find.

Other animals, such as the African bullfrog, **estivate** during dry times. To estivate is to spend the summer in a sleeplike state. These animals dig holes and rest inside them until rain falls.

Prairie dogs, mice, and gophers are rodents that live on grasslands. A rodent is a small animal with two large front teeth. Many rodents dig **burrows**. A burrow is an underground hole or tunnel where an animal lives. Earthworms also burrow. Burrowing creatures mix up soil nutrients as they dig. The digging lets air into the soil and allows spaces where the water can soak into the soil. These things help plants grow.

Different animals eat different parts of grassland plants. For example, zebras eat the tops of grass plants. Then, wildebeests eat the middles of the plants. Finally, Thomson's gazelles eat the bottoms of grass plants. Burrowing rodents can eat underground parts of plants. Birds eat plant seeds. In this way, there is enough food for many animals.

Scavengers eat animals they did not kill. Vultures, hyenas, and coyotes are some grassland scavengers. They help keep grasslands clean.

# Adaptation

Over millions of years, some animals have adapted to grassland life. Their bodies have changed to meet the needs of grassland living.

Grass is the most common grassland plant. But grass is a hard food for most animals to digest, or break down. Ruminants are animals that have adapted ways to better digest grass. They have a special part in their stomach called a rumen. Ruminants partly digest grasses in the rumen. They then bring this food back up into their mouths. Ruminants chew the food and swallow it again to finish digesting the grass.

Animals have also adapted to keep their young safe. For example, kangaroo mothers carry their young in pouches. Young kangaroos would be easy for carnivores to catch if they were not in the pouches.

Some grassland birds, such as the ostrich, cannot fly. But the ostrich has adapted. It has long, powerful legs. It can run very fast to escape from enemies. Ostriches can run up to 45 miles (72 km) per hour.

Kangaroos can live without drinking water for long periods of time.

Termite mounds can be up to 20 feet (6 m) high. Insects, birds, reptiles, and nesting animals often use the mounds as homes after termites leave them.

# Insects

Grasslands are home to many insects. Grassland insects include grasshoppers, termites, beetles, and ants. Insects help break down dead plants. This adds nutrients to the grassland soil.

Insects are important to the food chain of the grasslands. Small animals and birds feed on insects. Larger animals then feed on these smaller animals.

Insects are also important to plants. They help spread pollen. Pollen are tiny grains made in some flowers. Most plants need pollen from others of the same kind to make new plants.

Grasshoppers are among the most common grassland insects. They can eat almost any kind of plant. Some kinds of grasshoppers form swarms from time to time. A swarm is a huge group of insects. Locust is one kind of swarming grasshopper. A swarm of locusts eats everything in its path, including huge parts of grasslands.

Termites are the most common insects in tropical grasslands. They build tall mounds above ground to live in. After a time, they move and build new mounds. Termites eat mostly wood.

Huge herds of buffalo lived on the grasslands that once covered most of North America. Today, there are few wild buffalo. Many have died from overhunting and the loss of their home.

# GRASSLANDS AND PEOPLE

Large grasslands once covered every continent except Antarctica. Today, grasslands are becoming smaller. People have taken over much of this land.

Some ranchers raise animals, such as cows or horses. These animals can overgraze. If they eat too much grass, it might not grow back.

People turn grassland into farmland. Farmers take out the native plants in a grassland area. Then they plant crops, such as corn and wheat.

Sometimes farming can harm grasslands. Grass roots usually hold soil in place. Without grass roots, winds can carry away soil. The rich topsoil blows away until the soil cannot hold water. After many years, the grassland may turn into a desert.

This line of trees in a farming field forms a windbreak to stop soil loss. A windbreak lessens the flow of wind.

# Today and Tomorrow

In the United States, more than 150,000 square miles (388,498 square km) of grasslands have turned into desert. In some African countries, overgrazing is causing grasslands to become deserts. Grassland animals are losing their homes and dying out.

Today, people are trying to save grasslands. Some governments are setting aside pieces of grassland that cannot be farmed or used by ranchers for grazing animals. Grassland plants and animals can safely live in these places.

People are also trying to stop farmlands from turning into deserts. Most of the farmland was once grassland. To stop soil loss, people plant lines of bushes and trees. This stops strong winds from carrying away soil.

People can also practice limited irrigation on farmed grasslands. To **irrigate** is to pump extra water onto the dry soil. The extra water wets the soil and makes it heavier so it will not blow away.

People hope these actions will save grasslands. They want to stop grasslands from turning into deserts in the future.

# Glossary

**adapt** (uh-DAPT)—to change over time to fit in a special environment

**estivate** (ESS-ti-vayt)—to rest in a sleeplike state for the summer

**burrow** (BUR-oh)—a hole or tunnel in the ground where an animal lives

**climate** (KLYE-mit)—the usual weather in a place; climate includes the amount of rain that falls, usual wind speeds, and temperatures.

**drought** (DROUT)—a long period without rain

**equator** (i-KWAY-tur)—an imaginary line around the middle of a planet; the equator divides Earth into a northern and a southern half.

**grazer** (GRAY-zur)—an animal that feeds on growing grasses and other plants

**humus** (HYOO-muhss)—a dark, damp layer of soil made mainly of rotting plants and some animal remains

**irrigate** (IHR-uh-gate)—to use pipes or other means to bring water to dry land

**savanna** (suh-VAN-uh)—a tropical grassland

## Grassland Animal Printouts
http://www.enchantedlearning.com/biomes/
　　grassland/grassland.shtml

## Grasslands Biome
http://mbgnet.mobot.org/pfg/diverse/biomes/
　　grasslnd/index.htm

## The Prairie Enthusiasts
http://www.prairie.pressenter.com/

# Useful Addresses

## Grand Prairie Friends
P.O. Box 36
Urbana, IL 61803-0036

## Tallgrass Prairie National Preserve
National Park Trust
Route 1, P.O. Box 14
Strong City, KS 66869

# Index